# THE BLUES MINUS YOU

## BACKGROUNDS BY A JAZZ TRIO
## FOR USE BY MUSICIANS

CD 7007
Cass. 1011

**MMO CD 7007**
**MMO Cass. 1011**

**Music Minus One**

# THE BLUES MINUS YOU

Backgrounds by a Jazz Trio for use by Musicians
Written and Arranged by Mal Waldron

| Band Complete Version | | *Page Numbers* Instruments | | |
| --- | --- | --- | --- | --- |
| | | C Inst. | Bb Instr. | Bass Clef |
| 1 | The Twister | 3 | 7 | 11 |
| 2 | Empty Street | 3 | 7 | 11 |
| 3 | Dealin' | 4 | 8 | 12 |
| 4 | Blue Gene | 4 | 8 | 12 |
| 5 | Pedal Eyes | 4 | 8 | 12 |
| 6 | Blue Greens 'N' Beans | 5 | 9 | 13 |
| 7 | Hip Tip | 5 | 9 | 13 |
| 8 | Earthy | 6 | 10 | 14 |
| 9 | Gospel Truth | 6 | 10 | 14 |
| 10 | Wheelin' | 6 | 10 | 14 |

# THE TWISTER

MAL WALDRON

# EMPTY STREET

MAL WALDRON

7007

# DEALIN'

MAL WALDRON

# BLUE GENE

MAL WALDRON

# PEDAL EYES

MAL WALDRON

7007

4

# BLUE GREENS 'N' BEANS

MAL WALDRON

# HIP TIP

MAL WALDRON

7007

# EARTHY

C INSTRUMENTS

MAL WALDRON

# GOSPEL TRUTH

MAL WALDRON

# WHEELIN'

MAL WALDRON

7007

6

# THE TWISTER

Bb INSTRUMENTS

MAL WALDRON

# EMPTY STREET

MAL WALDRON

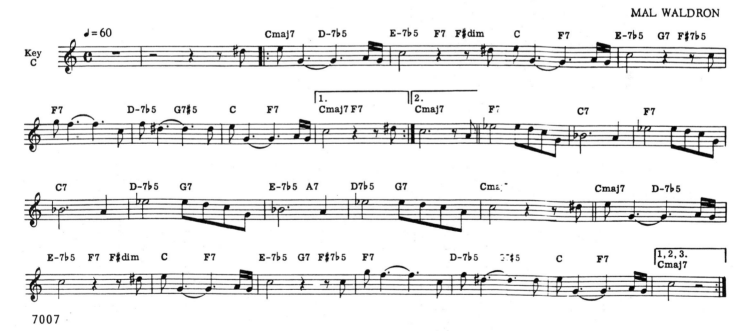

7007

# DEALIN'

MAL WALDRON

# BLUE GENE

MAL WALDRON

# PEDAL EYES

MAL WALDRON

7007

# BLUE GREENS 'N' BEANS

Bb INSTRUMENTS

MAL WALDRON

# HIP TIP

MAL WALDRON

7007

# EARTHY

MAL WALDRON

# GOSPEL TRUTH

MAL WALDRON

# WHEELIN'

MAL WALDRON

7007

# THE TWISTER

MAL WALDRON

# EMPTY STREET

MAL WALDRON

# DEALIN'

**Eb INSTRUMENTS**

MAL WALDRON

# BLUE GENE

MAL WALDRON

# PEDAL EYES

MAL WALDRON

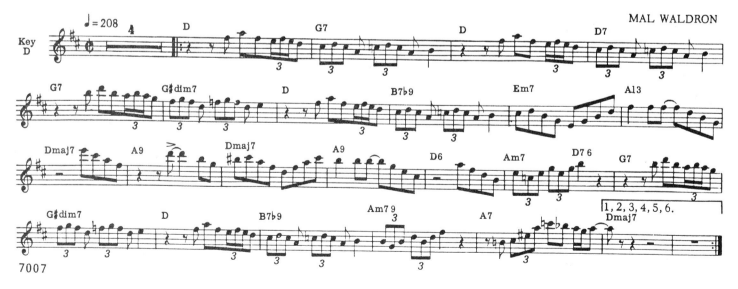

7007

12

# BLUE GREENS 'N' BEANS

MAL WALDRON

Eb INSTRUMENTS

# HIP TIP

MAL WALDRON

7007

# EARTHY

MAL WALDRON

# GOSPEL TRUTH

MAL WALDRON

# WHEELIN'

MAL WALDRON

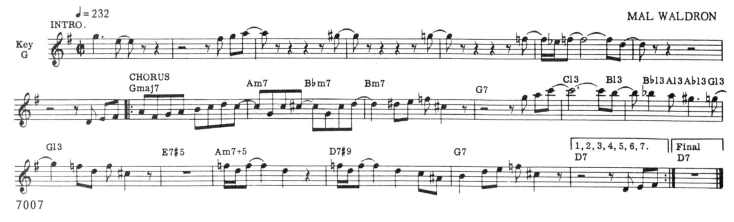

7007

14

| | | | |
|---|---|---|---|
| ___ | MMO CD | 3121 | 18th Century Violin Music with Orchestra |
| ___ | MMO CD | 3122 | Violin Favorites with Orchestra (easy) |
| ___ | MMO CD | 3123 | Violin Favorites with Orchestra (mod. difficult) |
| ___ | MMO CD | 3124 | Violin Favorites with Orchestra (mod. difficult) |
| ___ | MMO CD | 3125 | The Three B's: Bach, Beethoven and Brahms |
| ___ | MMO CD | 3126 | Vivaldi/Vivaldi/Vivaldi |
| ___ | MMO CD | 3127 | Vivaldi - The Four Seasons (2 CD set) |
| ___ | MMO CD | 3128 | Vivaldi Conc. Eb major, Albinoni Conc. A major |
| ___ | MMO CD | 3129 | Vivaldi Concerto in E & C Major |
| ___ | MMO CD | 3130 | Schubert Sonatinas |
| ___ | MMO CD | 3131 | Haydn String Quartet No. 1 in G major |
| ___ | MMO CD | 3132 | Haydn String Quartet No. 2 in D minor |
| ___ | MMO CD | 3133 | Haydn String Quartet No. 3 in C major |
| ___ | MMO CD | 3134 | Haydn String Quartet No. 4 in Bb major |
| ___ | MMO CD | 3135 | Haydn String Quartet No. 5 in D major |
| ___ | MMO CD | 3136 | Haydn String Quartet No. 6 in Eb major |

## Music Minus One CLARINET Compact Discs

| | | | |
|---|---|---|---|
| ___ | MMO CD | 3201 | Mozart Clarinet Concerto in A Major |
| ___ | MMO CD | 3202 | Weber/Stamitz Clarinet Concerti |
| ___ | MMO CD | 3203 | Spohr Concerto No.1 in C minor |
| ___ | MMO CD | 3204 | Weber Concertino/Beethoven Trio |
| ___ | MMO CD | 3205 | First Chair Clarinet Solos Orchestral Excerpts |
| ___ | MiMO CD | 3206 | The Art of the Solo Clarinet Orchestral Excerpts |
| ___ | MMO CD | 3207 | Mozart Clarinet Quintet in A major |
| ___ | MMO CD | 3208 | Brahms Sonatas Opus 120, # 1 & #2 |
| ___ | MMO CD | 3209 | Weber: Grand Duo Concertant - Wagner: Adagio |
| ___ | MMO CD | 3210 | Schumann Fantasy Pieces, Three Romances |
| ___ | MMO CD | 3211 | Easy Clarinet Solos, Student Series, 1-3 years |
| ___ | MMO CD | 3212 | Easy Clarinet Solos, Vol. 2 |
| ___ | MMO CD | 3213 | Easy Jazz Duets |

Choice selections for the Clarinet, drawn from the very best solo literature for the instrument. The pieces are performed by the foremost virtuosi of our time, artists affiliated with the New York Philharmonic, Boston, Chicago, Cleveland and Philadelphia Orchestras. The Julliard School, Curtis Institute of Music, Indiana University, University of Toronto and Metropolitan Opera Ochestra.

| | | | |
|---|---|---|---|
| ___ | MMO CD | 3221 | Jerome Bunke, Clinician - Beginning Level |
| ___ | MMO CD | 3222 | Beginning Contest Solos - Harold Wright |
| ___ | MMO CD | 3223 | Intermediate Contest Solos - Stanley Drucker |
| ___ | MMO CD | 3224 | Intermediate Contest Solos - Julius Baker |
| ___ | MMO CD | 3225 | Advanced Contest Solos - Stanley Drucker |
| ___ | MMO CD | 3226 | Advanced Contest Solos - Harold Wright |
| ___ | MMO CD | 3227 | Intermediate Contest Solos - Stanley Drucker |
| ___ | MMO CD | 3228 | Advanced Contest Solos - Stanley Drucker |
| ___ | MMO CD | 3229 | Advanced Contest Solos - Harold Wright |

## Music Minus One FLUTE Compact Discs

| | | | |
|---|---|---|---|
| ___ | MMO CD | 3300 | Mozart Concerto in D, Quantz Concerto in G |
| ___ | MMO CD | 3301 | Mozart Concerto in G |
| ___ | MMO CD | 3302 | J.S. Bach Suite #2 in Bm |
| ___ | MMO CD | 3303 | Boccherini in D, Vivaldi #2 in Gm, Mozart Andante |
| ___ | MMO CD | 3304 | Haydn, Vivaldi, Frederick "The Great" Concertos |
| ___ | MMO CD | 3305 | Vivaldi in F, Telemann in D, LeClair in C Concertos |
| ___ | MMO CD | 3306 | Bach Brandenburg Concerto #2, Haydn Conc. in D |
| ___ | MMO CD | 3307 | Bach "Triple' Concerto in Am, Vivaldi #9 in Dm |
| ___ | MMO CD | 3308 | Mozart Quartet in F, Stamitz Quartet in F |
| ___ | MMO CD | 3309 | Haydn London Trios |
| ___ | MMO CD | 3310 | Bach Brandenburg Concerti #4 & #5 |
| ___ | MMO CD | 3311 | Mozart Three Flute Quartets, C - D - A major |
| ___ | MMO CD | 3313 | Flute Song |
| ___ | MMO CD | 3314 | Vivaldi Concerto in D major, G major, F major |
| ___ | MMO CD | 3315 | Vivaldi Concerto in Am, G, D |
| ___ | MMO CD | 3316 | Easy Flute Solos, Student Series, Beginning Level |
| ___ | MMO CD | 3317 | Easy Flute Solos, Student Series, Vol.2 |
| ___ | MMO CD | 3318 | Easy Jazz Duets |
| ___ | MMO CD | 3319 | Flute and Guitar Duets Vol. 1 |
| ___ | MMO CD | 3320 | Flute and Guitar Duets Vol. 2 |
| ___ | MMO CD | 3333 | First Chair Solos |

Choice sections for the Flute, drawn from the very best solo literature for the instrument. The pieces are performed by the foremost virtuosi of our time, artists affiliated with the New York Philharmonic, Boston, Chicago, Cleveland and Philadelphia Orchestras. The Julliard School, Curtis Institute of Music, Indiana University, University of Toronto and Metropolitan Opera Orchestra.

| | | | |
|---|---|---|---|
| ___ | MMO CD | 3321 | Murray Panitz, Philadelphia Orch - Beginning |
| ___ | MMO CD | 3322 | Beginning Contest Solos - Donald Peck |
| ___ | MMO CD | 3323 | Julius Baker, NY Philharmonic - Intermediate |
| ___ | MMO CD | 3324 | Intermediate Contest Solos - Donald Peck |

| | | | |
|---|---|---|---|
| ___ | MMO CD | 3325 | Murray Panitz, Philadelphia Orch - Advanced |
| ___ | MMO CD | 3326 | Advanced Contest Solos - Julius Baker |
| ___ | MMO CD | 3327 | Intermediate Contest Solos - Donald Peck |
| ___ | MMO CD | 3328 | Murray Panitz, Philadelphia Orch - Beginning |
| ___ | MMO CD | 3329 | Julius Baker, NY Philharmonic - Intermediate |
| ___ | MMO CD | 3330 | Doriot Anthony Dwyer, Boston Symphony- Beginning |
| ___ | MMO CD | 3331 | Doriot Anthony Dwyer, Boston Symphony - Intermed. |
| ___ | MMO CD | 3332 | Doriot Anthony Dwyer, Boston Symphony - Advanced |

## Music Minus One OBOE Compact Discs

| | | | |
|---|---|---|---|
| ___ | MMO CD | 3400 | Albinoni Concerto Bb, D, & Dm |
| ___ | MMO CD | 3401 | Telemann F minor, Handel #8 Bb major, Vivaldi #9 |
| ___ | MMO CD | 3402 | Mozart Quartet F major, Stamitz Quartet F major |

## Music Minus One FRENCH HORN Compact Discs

| | | | |
|---|---|---|---|
| ___ | MMO CD | 3501 | Mozart Concert i No.2 & No.3 |
| ___ | MMO CD | 3502 | Baroque Brass and Beyond, Brass Quintet |
| ___ | MMO CD | 3503 | Music For Brass Quintet |

Choice selections for the French Horn, drawn from the very best solo literature for the instrument. The pieces are performed by the foremost virtuosi of our time, artists affiliated with the New York Philharmonic, Boston, Chicago, Cleveland and Philadelphia Orchestras. The Julliard School, Curtis Institute of Music, Indiana University, University of Toronto and Metropolitan opera Orchestra.

| | | | |
|---|---|---|---|
| ___ | MMO CD | 3511 | Beginning Contest Solos |
| ___ | MMO CD | 3512 | Beginning Contest Solos |
| ___ | MMO CD | 3513 | Dale Clevenger, Chicago Symphony - Intermediate |
| ___ | MMO CD | 3514 | Mason Jones, Philadelphia Orchestra - Intermediate |
| ___ | MMO CD | 3515 | Myron Bloom, Cleveland Symphony - Advanced |
| ___ | MMO CD | 3516 | Dale Clevenger, Chicago Symphony - Intermediate |
| ___ | MMO CD | 3517 | Mason Jones, Philadelphia Orchestra - Intermediate |
| ___ | MMO CD | 3518 | Myron Bloom, Cleveland Symphony - Advanced |
| ___ | MMO CD | 3519 | Dale Clevenger, Chicago Symphony - Intermediate |

## Music Minus One CELLO Compact Discs

| | | | |
|---|---|---|---|
| ___ | MMO CD | 3701 | DVORAK Concerto in B Minor |
| ___ | MMO CD | 3702 | C.P.E. Bach Concerto in A minor |
| ___ | MMO CD | 3703 | Boccherini Conc. in Bb, Bruch Kol Nidrei |
| ___ | MMO CD | 3704 | Schumann Concerti Plus Three More |
| ___ | MMO CD | 3705 | Ten Pieces For Cello and Piano |
| ___ | MMO CD | 3706 | Claude Bolling Suite for Cello and Jazz Piano Trio |

## Music Minus One TRUMPET Compact Discs

| | | | |
|---|---|---|---|
| ___ | MMO CD | 3801 | Three Trumpet Concerti |
| ___ | MMO CD | 3802 | Easy Trumpet Solos, Student Series, Beg. Level |
| ___ | MMO CD | 3803 | Easy Trumpet Solos, Student Series, Vol.2 |
| ___ | MMO CD | 3804 | Easy Jazz Duets For Trumpets |
| ___ | MMO CD | 3805 | Music For Brass Ensemble |
| ___ | MMO CD | 3806 | First Chair Trumpet Solos Orchestral Excerpts |
| ___ | MMO CD | 3807 | The Art Of Solo Trumpet |
| ___ | MMO CD | 3808 | Baroque, Brass, And Beyond |
| ___ | MMO CD | 3809 | The Arban Trumpet Duets |
| ___ | MMO CD | 3810 | Sousa Marches and Beethoven/Strauss/Berlioz |

Choice selections for the Trumpet, drawn from the very best solo literature for the instrument. The pieces are performed by the foremost virtuosi of our time, artists affiliated with the New York Philharmonic, Boston, Chicago, Cleveland and Philadelphia Orchestras. The Julliard School, Curtis Institute of Music, Indiana University, University of Toronto and Metropolitan Opera Orchestra.

| | | | |
|---|---|---|---|
| ___ | MMO CD | 3811 | Beginning Contest Solos |
| ___ | MMO CD | 3812 | Beginning Contest Solos |
| ___ | MMO CD | 3813 | Intermediate Contest Solos |
| ___ | MMO CD | 3814 | Intermediate Contest Solos |
| ___ | MMO CD | 3815 | Advanced Contest Solos |
| ___ | MMO CD | 3816 | Advanced Contest Solos |
| ___ | MMO CD | 3817 | Intermediate Contest Solos |
| ___ | MMO CD | 3818 | Advanced Contest Solos |
| ___ | MMO CD | 3819 | Advanced Contest Solos |
| ___ | MMO CD | 3821 | Beginning Contest Solos |
| ___ | MMO CD | 3822 | Intermediate Contest Solos |

## Music Minus One TROMBONE Compact Discs

|   | MMO CD | 3901 | Easy Solos, Student Series, Beginning Level |
|---|--------|------|---|
|   | MMO CD | 3902 | Easy Solos, Student Series. Beg/Intermediate Level |
|   | MMO CD | 3903 | Easy Jazz Duets, 1-3rd Student Level |
|   | MMO CD | 3904 | Baroque, Brass & Beyond - Brass Quintet Music |
|   | MMO CD | 3905 | Music For Brass Ensemble |

Choice selections for the Trombone, drawn from the very best solo literature for the instrument. The pieces are performed by the foremost virtuosi of our time, artists affiliated with the New York Philharmonic, Boston, Chicago, Cleveland and Philadelphia Orchestras. The Julliard School, Curtis Institute of Music, Indiana University, University of Toronto and Metropolitan Opera Orchestra.

|   | MMO CD | 3911 | Beginning Contest Solos |
|---|--------|------|---|
|   | MMO CD | 3912 | Beginning Contest Solos |
|   | MMO CD | 3913 | Keith Brown, Professor, Indiana University - Intermediate |
|   | MMO CD | 3914 | Jay Friedman, Chicago Symphony - Intermediate |
|   | MMO CD | 3915 | Keith Brown, Professor, Indiana University - Advanced |
|   | MMO CD | 3916 | Per Brevig, Metropolitan Opera - Advanced |
|   | MMO CD | 3917 | Keith Brown, Professor, Indiana University - Advanced |
|   | MMO CD | 3918 | Jay Friedman, Chicago Symphony - Advanced |
|   | MMO CD | 3919 | Per Brevig, Metropolitan Opera - Advanced |

## Music Minus One VOCALIST Compact Discs

|   | MMO CD | 4001 | Schubert German Lieder for High Voice |
|---|--------|------|---|
|   | MMO CD | 4002 | Schubert German Lieder for Low Voice |
|   | MMO CD | 4003 | Schubert German Lieder, Vol. 2, for High Voice |
|   | MMO CD | 4004 | Schubert German Lieder, Vol. 2, for Low Voice |
|   | MMO CD | 4005 | Brahms German Lieder for High Voice |
|   | MMO CD | 4006 | Brahms German Lieder for Low Voice |
|   | MMO CD | 4007 | Everybody's Favorite Songs for High Voice |
|   | MMO CD | 4008 | Everybody's Favorite Songs for Low Voice |
|   | MMO CD | 4009 | Everybody's Favorite Songs, Vol. 2, High Voice |
|   | MMO CD | 4010 | Everybody's Favorite Songs, Vol. 2 Low Voice |
|   | MMO CD | 4011 | 17th/18th Century Italian songs High Voice |
|   | MMO CD | 4012 | 17th/18th Century Italian songs Low Voice |
|   | MMO CD | 4013 | 17th/18th Century Italian songs #2 High Voice |
|   | MMO CD | 4014 | 17th/18th Century Italian songs #2 Low Voice |
|   | MMO CD | 4015 | Famous Soprano Arias |
|   | MMO CD | 4016 | Famous Mezzo-Soprano Arias |
|   | MMO CD | 4017 | Famous Tenor Arias |
|   | MMO CD | 4018 | Famous Baritone Arias |
|   | MMO CD | 4019 | Famous Bass Arias |
|   | MMO CD | 4020 | Wolf German Lieder For High Voice |
|   | MMO CD | 4021 | Wolf German Lieder For Low Voice |
|   | MMO CD | 4022 | Strauss German Lieder For High Voice |
|   | MMO CD | 4023 | Strauss German Lieder For Low Voice |
|   | MMO CD | 4024 | Schumann German Lieder for High Voice |
|   | MMO CD | 4025 | Schumann German Lieder for Low Voice |
|   | MMO CD | 4026 | Mozart Arias for Soprano |
|   | MMO CD | 4027 | Verdi Arias for Soprano |
|   | MMO CD | 4028 | Italian Arias For Soprano |
|   | MMO CD | 4029 | French Arias For Soprano |
|   | MMO CD | 4030 | Soprano Oratorio Arias |
|   | MMO CD | 4031 | Alto Oratorio Arias |
|   | MMO CD | 4032 | Tenor Oratorio Arias |
|   | MMO CD | 4033 | Bass Oratorio Arias |

In a field which is dominated by the vocal soloist, John Wustman is one of the few accompanists in this country who has achieved renown and critical acclaim in this most challenging of art forms. Mr. Wustman has developed that rare quality of bringing a strength and character to his accompaniments which create a true collaboration between the singer and the pianist. And this is as it should be, for in the art song especially, the piano part is not a mere rhythmic and tonal background, but an integral part of the composer's intent and creation. Thus, on these records, Mr. Wustman provides not only the necessary accompaniment but also through his artistry a stylistic and interpretive suggestion for the study of music. Among the many artists he has accompanied in the past years are: Gianna d'Angelo, Irina Arkhipova, Montserrat Caballe, Regine Crespin, Nicolai Gedda, Evelyn Lear, Mildred Miller, Anna Moffo, Birgit Nilsson, Jan Peerce, Roberta Peters, Elisabeth Schwarzkopf, Renata Scotto, Cesare Siepi, Giulietta Simionato, Thoms Stewart, Cesare Valetti and William Warfield. Mr. Wustman has become known to millions of television viewers as the accompanist to Luciano Pavarotti in his many appearances in that medium.

Choice selections for the Vocalist, drawn from the very best solo literature for the voice. Professional artists perform these pieces to guide the singer in interpreting each piece.

|   | MMO CD | 4041 | Beginning Soprano Solos - Kate Hurney |
|---|--------|------|---|
|   | MMO CD | 4042 | Intermediate Soprano Solos - Kate Hurney |
|   | MMO CD | 4043 | Beginning Mezzo Soprano Solos - Fay Kittelson |
|   | MMO CD | 4044 | Intermediate Mezzo Soprano Solos - Fay Kittelson |
|   | MMO CD | 4045 | Advanced Mezzo Soprano Solos - Fay Kittelson |
|   | MMO CD | 4046 | Beginning Contralto Solos - Carline Ray |
|   | MMO CD | 4047 | Beginning Tenor Solos - George Shirley |
|   | MMO CD | 4048 | Intermediate Tenor Solos - George Shirley |
|   | MMO CD | 4049 | Advanced Tenor Solos - George Shirley |

## Music Minus One GUITAR Compact Discs

|   | MMO CD | 3601 | Boccherini: Guitar Quintet, No.4 in D major |
|---|--------|------|---|
|   | MMO CD | 3602 | Giuliani: Guitar Quintet in A Major |
|   | MMO CD | 3603 | Classic Guitar Duets Easy-Medium |
|   | MMO CD | 3604 | Renaissance & Baroque for Two Guitars |
|   | MMO CD | 3605 | Classical & Romantic Guitar Duets |
|   | MMO CD | 3606 | Guitar and Flute Duets Vol. 1 |
|   | MMO CD | 3607 | Guitar and Flute Duets Vol. 2 |
|   | MMO CD | 3608 | Bluegrass Guitar |
|   | MMO CD | 3609 | George Barne's Guitar Method |
|   | MMO CD | 3610 | How To Play Folk Guitar |
|   | MMO CD | 3611 | Favorite Folk Songs For Guitar |
|   | MMO CD | 3612 | Jimmy Raney/Jack Wilkins Jam Guitar Sounds |
|   | MMO CD | 3613 | Barnes & Kress Guitar Duets |

## Music Minus One BANJO Compact Discs

|   | MMO CD | 4401 | Bluegrass Banjo |
|---|--------|------|---|
|   | MMO CD | 4402 | Play The Five String Banjo Vol. 1 |
|   | MMO CD | 4403 | Five String Banjo Method Vol. 2 |

## Music Minus One TENOR SAX Compact Discs

|   | MMO CD | 4201 | Easy Tenor/Sopr. Solos, Student Series, Beg. Level |
|---|--------|------|---|
|   | MMO CD | 4202 | Easy Tenor/Sopr. Solos, Student Series, Vol.2 |
|   | MMO CD | 4203 | Easy Jazz Duets For Tenor Sax |
|   | MMO CD | 4204 | For Saxes Only - Arranged by Bob Wilber |

## Music Minus One ALTO SAX Compact Discs

|   | MMO CD | 4101 | Easy Alto Sax Solos, Student Series, Beg. Level |
|---|--------|------|---|
|   | MMO CD | 4102 | Easy Alto Sax Solos, Student Series, Vol.2 |
|   | MMO CD | 4103 | Easy Jazz Duets For Alto Sax |
|   | MMO CD | 4104 | For Saxes Only - Arranged by Bob Wilber |

Choice selections for the Alto Sax, drawn from the very best solo literature for the instrument. The pieces are performed by the foremost virtuosi of our time, artists affiliated with the New York Philharmonic, Boston, Chicago, Cleveland and Philadelphia Orchestras. The Julliard School, Curtis Institute of Music, Indiana University, University of Toronto and Metropolitan Opera Orchestra.

|   | MMO CD | 4111 | Paul Bordie, Canadian Soloist, Beginning |
|---|--------|------|---|
|   | MMO CD | 4112 | Vincent Abato, Metropolitan Orch. - Beginning |
|   | MMO CD | 4113 | Paul Brodie, Canadian Soloist - Intermediate |
|   | MMO CD | 4114 | Vincent Abato, Metropolitan Opera - Intermediate |
|   | MMO CD | 4115 | Paul Brodie, Canadian Soloist - Advanced |
|   | MMO CD | 4116 | Vincent Abato, Metropolitan Opera - Advanced |
|   | MMO CD | 4117 | Paul Brodie, Canadian Soloist - Advanced |
|   | MMO CD | 4118 | Vincent Abato, Metropolitan Opera - Advanced |

## Music Minus One DOUBLE BASS Compact Discs

|   | MMO CD | 4301 | David Walter, Julliard School, Beg-Intermediate |
|---|--------|------|---|
|   | MMO CD | 4302 | David Walter, Julliard School, Intermediate-Adv. |
|   | MMO CD | 4303 | For Bassists Only |
|   | MMO CD | 4304 | The Beat Goes On - Jazz-Funk, Latin, Pop-Rock |

## Music Minus One DRUMS Compact Discs

|   | MMO CD | 5001 | Modern Jazz Drumming (2 CD Set) |
|---|--------|------|---|
|   | MMO CD | 5002 | For Drummers Only! |
|   | MMO CD | 5003 | Wipe Out |
|   | MMO CD | 5004 | Sit-in with Jim Chapin |
|   | MMO CD | 5005 | Drum Star |
|   | MMO CD | 5006 | Drumpadstickskin |
|   | MMO CD | 5009 | Classical Percussion, 2 CD set |
|   | MMO CD | 5010 | Eight Men in Search of a Drummer |